THE ANCIENT WORLD

ANCIENT GREECE

BY PETER BENOIT

CHILDREN'S PRESS®
AN IMPRINT OF SCHOLASTIC INC.
NEW YORK TORONTO LONDON AUCKLAND SYDNEY
MEXICO CITY NEW DELHI HONG KONG
DANBURY, CONNECTICUT

Content Consultant
Laura Gawlinski, PhD,
Assistant Professor,
Loyola University Chicago

Library of Congress Cataloging-in-Publication Data
Benoit, Peter, 1955–
  Ancient Greece/by Peter Benoit.
    p. cm.—(The Ancient World)
  Includes bibliographical references and index.
  ISBN: 978-0-531-25178-2 (lib. bdg.)   ISBN: 978-0-531-25978-8 (pbk.)
  1. Greece—Civilization—To 146 B.C.—Juvenile literature. I. Title.
  DF77.B526 2013
  938—dc23   2012000507

JOURNEY BACK TO ANCIENT GREECE

The ancient Greeks were the first people to practice democratic government.

The first people settled in what became Greece as early as 128,000 BCE.

Many modern buildings have been heavily influenced by ancient Greek architecture.

TABLE OF CONTENTS

An ancient Greek helmet

A Mycenaean vase

THE SEEDS OF GREATNESS

Without the unique and enduring **legacy** of ancient Greece, we would live in a different world. Our buildings would not be the same. There would be no graceful columns outside nor spiral staircases inside the buildings. Our paintings and sculptures would look vastly different. Additionally, our ancestors

The columns that we see on many buildings today were inspired by the work of ancient Greek architects.

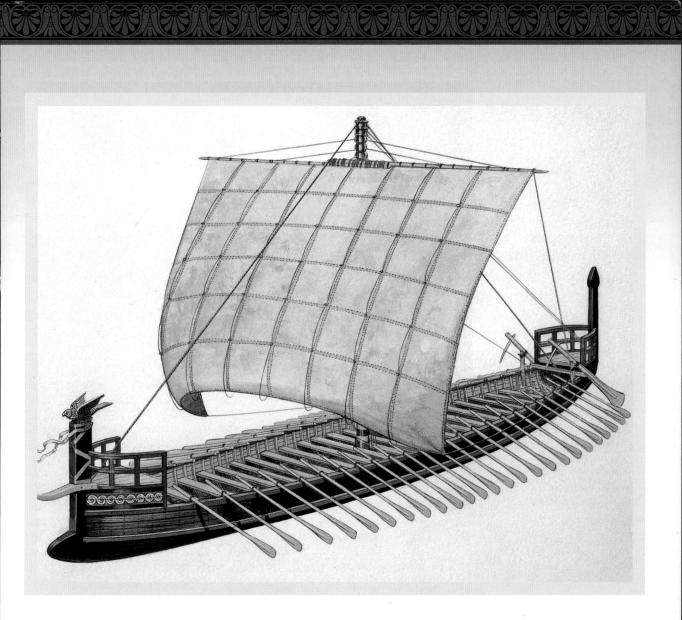

would not have benefited from many basic technologies, because the ideas for them originated in ancient Greece. There would have been no cranes or winches to lift heavy objects. Plumbing systems would not have been as refined. Water would not have been used with such imagination in water mills and water clocks. The ancient Greeks also gave the world useful inventions such as three-masted ships, canal locks, and devices that predict eclipses.

Early ships had just one or two masts.

legacy (LEG-uh-see) something handed down from one generation to another

Without Solon's contributions, many governments might be very different today.

Renaissance (REN-uh-sahns) the revival of art and learning, inspired by the ancient Greeks and Romans, that took place in Europe between the fourteenth and sixteenth centuries

The influence of ancient Greece is also seen in our philosophy and literature. Without the greatness of Greek philosophers, we might not have the same principles for living our lives. We would not appreciate the middle ground between extremes, an idea that shaped many cultures after the passing of classical Greece. Without colonization, warfare, and trade, the ideas that shaped Greek culture would never have extended much beyond the shores of mainland Greece. There would have been no influence on Rome and no **Renaissance** in Europe centuries later, the foundation on which Western civilization rests.

It's easy to forget that before the political reforms of Solon and Cleisthenes in Athens twenty-five hundred years ago, there was no democracy. Instead, political power lay exclusively in the hands of the aristocracy. Under Solon, Athenian citizens were for the first time considered, at least in theory, equal before the law. Many modern nations owe the principles of their governments to these humble beginnings.

The Greek accomplishments in science and mathematics have had a long-lasting effect on Western society. The Greeks used mathematics to analyze **abstract** concepts. This affected not only progress within mathematics, but also in science and even in politics. As a result, critical analysis expanded to include all fields of study. Only a few conclusions reached by these early Greek scientists have survived, and most have been revised many times. But the critical, questioning mind embodied by the ancient Greeks still lives on.

Greek philosophers such as Aristotle have greatly influenced the way we think about the world.

abstract (ab-STRAKT) based on ideas rather than things you can touch and see

CHAPTER ONE

A GREAT CIVILIZATION IS BORN

istorians often think of ancient Greece as beginning with the rise of city-states and the colonization of the region around the Mediterranean Sea in about 750 BCE. The closing of the Neoplatonic Academy in 529 CE often marks the end of ancient Greece, although some historians use other dates. Archaeologists, however, recognize that Greek civilization is much older. As early as 128,000 BCE, settlers from western Turkey and the Middle East established small communities on the shores of Crete. This island lies in the Mediterranean Sea south of

The Minoans formed the roots of the civilization that would grow to become ancient Greece.

present-day Greece. The first farming communities on Crete were not established until about 7000 BCE. This Minoan civilization, as it eventually came to be known, was a society based on extended families and clans living in villages.

Archaeologists have learned about the Minoans by studying ruins on Crete.

The Past Is Present
A QUESTION OF OWNERSHIP

The Parthenon, a temple dedicated to the Greek goddess Athena, is a lasting symbol of ancient Greece and democracy, as well as being one of the world's most magnificent structures. Built between 447 and 432 BCE, the Parthenon replaced an earlier temple of Athena that was destroyed during the Persian invasion in 480 BCE. The building was originally decorated with hundreds of sculptures of gods and mythological and historical figures. In the early nineteenth century, the Earl of Elgin, of England, had the sculptures removed and put

on display at the British Museum in London. Today, an argument rages between the Greek government, which wants the sculptures returned, and the museum, which claims it has the proper legal rights to keep the sculptures. The outcome of the debate will affect thousands of museum collections throughout the world.

As agriculture became more sophisticated, beginning about 5000 BCE, the population grew. The Minoans gradually expanded sea trade with other groups in the Aegean Sea. On Cyprus, south of present-day Turkey, the commercial center of Akrotiri had grown to about ten thousand people by 2000 BCE. This growth was based in part on trade with the Minoans. By around this time, the Minoans were building grand palaces that probably served as centers for religious ceremonies. They were manufacturing richly designed, eggshell-thin pottery and making delicate gold jewelry. They also began to trade extensively with groups on the Greek mainland.

Some Minoans may have worshipped a snake goddess.

Then disaster struck. In the seventeenth century BCE, an earthquake shook the great palaces of Crete. Then, in about 1627 BCE, a volcano on the Aegean island of Thera erupted. Although the major Minoan towns were spared total devastation, the volcano caused huge tidal waves and left the Minoans open for attack by invaders. Whatever damage was caused seems to have been soon repaired. Over the next two or three centuries, palaces at Knossos, Phaistos, and Malia were all restored to their former glory.

Minoan society now reached its peak. With the Old Palace period at an end, a new age of prosperity began. Larger towns were built, and the wealthy constructed impressive, sprawling villas for themselves. **Cult** and other religious worship became

cult (KUHLT) the religious worship of a specific deity

Mycenaean pottery was often painted with beautiful designs.

opium (OH-pee-uhm) a powerful drug made from poppies, from which heroin and morphine are made

fortified (FOR-tuh-fyed) stronger and providing better protection from attack

more elaborate. Evidence indicates that some Minoans may have taken part in a snake cult, and there is proof of at least one example of human sacrifice. In some places, **opium** was used at religious ceremonies, and some Minoans worshipped a poppy goddess.

Minoan influences, as well as trade with Crete, had made an impact throughout the southern Aegean, the Greek mainland, and Egypt. By 1450 BCE, however, Minoan civilization was about to face its greatest challenge.

The Mycenaeans— Conquest and Collapse

In 1450 BCE, Crete was rocked by a massive earthquake, which greatly weakened the Minoan civilization. Within twenty-five years, the Mycenaeans, conquerors from mainland Greece, occupied the Minoan palaces. They borrowed heavily from the Minoan system of writing to make their own. For years before their conquest of Crete, the Mycenaeans had been expanding their influence throughout the Aegean. They traded wool, wine, and olive oil for copper and tin, which they used to make durable bronze weapons. The Mycenaeans built huge, **fortified** walls of limestone, unlike the Minoans, who had lived in unfortified towns. In Minoan society, the priests were the upper class. The Mycenaeans, however, glorified the warrior class.

Warriors occupied a respected position in Mycenaean society.

Archaeologists have found evidence in Mycenaean religion of many gods and goddesses associated with classical Greece. They include Athena, Aphrodite, and Ares, with the sea god, Poseidon, atop the **pantheon**. According to legend, black bulls were sacrificed to Poseidon at Pylos, a city on the southwestern coast of the mainland. Pylos was a major trade center, connected by common interests with merchants and ruling aristocrats at Tiryns, Mycenae, and Athens. On Crete, the Mycenaeans sometimes worshipped in holy places established centuries earlier by the Minoans.

By 1200 BCE, the palace of Pylos was burned by invaders and lay in ruins. Some Mycenaean towns, including Athens, suffered little damage at the hands of invaders. However, over the next centuries, Mycenaean culture declined. Gold and silver objects were no longer produced, and handsome palace paintings were no longer created. Trade in tin was halted, and the manufacturing of bronze, which required tin, ceased. The Greeks turned instead to local deposits of iron ore and began making weapons with iron. People were no longer taught to read or write, and communities became isolated as trade ended. Greece entered a grim period for three centuries and would not emerge until about 800 BCE.

During this period, called the Greek Dark Age, people migrated and settled in other regions. There was widespread cultural change. Ethnic groups established new colonies and spoke different forms of the language. Archaeologists still find evidence of wealth and status in burial mounds, however, with women occasionally wearing gold. As agricultural settlements slowly began to prosper, trade with groups from the East increased. Greeks in the Dark Age sometimes traded slaves for gold, textiles, and ivory. Yet the pace of recovery was slow—until a dramatic turnabout in the eighth century BCE.

Athena (left) and Poseidon (right) were two of the most important deities in the ancient Greek religion.

Pottery grew more complex during the Archaic period.

THE MIRACLE OF ARCHAIC GREECE (750–500 BCE)

The thirteen centuries stretching from approximately 750 BCE to 529 CE saw the full flowering of classical Greek civilization. The early part of this period is known as **Archaic** Greece. This cultural rebirth was accompanied by increasing population, improvements in shipbuilding that expanded trade, and higher agricultural production.

Early Dark Age pottery had been small and simple, using basic geometric shapes as decoration. The size of pots, and the complexity and variety of their patterns, began to increase before the Greek

archaic (ahr-KAY-ik) from the past and not used anymore

18

rebirth. The presence of certain patterns and designs indicate that the Greeks had broadened their trade networks. Some of the designs may have been consciously patterned on those of textiles. Aside from a handful of earlier examples, human figures on pottery were introduced in the 700s BCE. The largest pots, made to honor heroes slain in battle, are nearly 5 feet (1.5 meters) tall. Some pots show full battle scenes.

The first phase of the Greek rebirth was also marked by the appearance of a new and flexible alphabet. The Greeks began to use the Phoenician alphabet, modifying it to suit their purposes. The new script was often used to **inscribe** offerings to the gods, usually with the name of the person making the offering and the god to whom it was made. In addition, the script was used to record commercial dealings, thereby helping to build trade. It could also be used to record the oral traditions of Greece's Dark Age authors.

This period witnessed the rise of the city-state, or polis. Eventually, there would be hundreds of them. City-states strengthened local loyalties and provided an opportunity to create a fairer, more balanced society. City-states adopted gods whom they looked to for protection, and altars and temples were built to worship

inscribe (in-SKRIBE) to write, carve, or engrave letters on a surface

The Phoenician alphabet formed the basis of ancient Greek writing.

the gods. Athens and Sparta built temples to Athena, Corinth built temples to Apollo, and Samos built them to Hera. As city-states accumulated more wealth, they competed with one another to build the grandest temple. As populations boomed by the sixth century BCE, city-states constructed paved streets and built fountains and large public buildings. Each city-state maintained its own army to protect its border.

Many city-states featured impressive buildings and paved streets.

As the population increased, Greek culture was affected from top to bottom. It fostered the rise of a **mercantile** class. The growing population created land shortages, which put wealthy landowners in conflict with the poor. Merchants, now with a path to wealth and influence, stood as a threat to the aristocracy. Merchants demanded political power, and internal conflict was common.

City-states fought with one another for control of important agricultural resources. In around 700 BCE, Chalcis and Eretria fought for control of the fertile Lelantine Plain, which lay between them on the island of Euboea off the eastern coast of present-day Greece. The conflict drew other city-states into the war, as one after another took sides in the ongoing fighting. Though Chalcis won control, both it and Eretria were weakened. Corinth, meanwhile, grew in stature and influence as a result of the Lelantine War, absorbing much of Chalcis.

In the first Messenian War, Sparta battled with Messenia for nearly twenty years, finally defeating the city-state in about 724 BCE. Many surviving Messenians fled to other city-states. Those who did not flee were forced to become **helots**, working the land and supporting the citizens of Sparta. Sparta changed rapidly and became an even more powerful military force. Sparta's male citizens were now obligated to serve as soldiers.

Meanwhile, Athens experienced widespread social unrest. Because each of Athens's sixty aristocratic clans participated in the election of the city-state's ruling judges, or archons, the clans often jockeyed for power. After their term in office, archons would take their place in the Council of the Areopagus, which controlled political life in Athens. In addition, each clan controlled territory on the Attic Peninsula, which projects into the Aegean, and land

mercantile (MUR-kan-tile) relating to trade

helots (HEL-uhts) members of a class of serfs in ancient Sparta

disputes inevitably arose. In a failed revolt led by the aristocrat Cylon in 632 BCE, the rival clan of the victorious Alcmaeonids moved to have Cylon's clan slaughtered, even though it had sought protection at a temple of the gods. The other clans considered this an outrage and expelled the Alcmaeonids from the Attic Peninsula. The Alcmaeonids' buried ancestors were removed from their graves and their remains were placed beyond the boundary of Attica to calm the angry gods.

Some city-states, such as Sparta, were especially aggressive in attacking foreign city-states.

Conflict between clans was only one of several crises that Athens faced during the Archaic period. The expanding population of Athens caused food shortages. To solve the crisis, Athens established grain-exporting colonies on the Black Sea and northern Aegean Sea. Colonization brought the Athenians into conflict with earlier and better established groups. Additionally, being at the mercy of winds and sudden storms at sea, the seafaring Athenians were always at risk of being shipwrecked.

Ships faced great danger from storms when they sailed out to sea.

23

Solon's changes to Athenian government included greater involvement of common citizens.

Colonization resulted in expansion of trade with the East. This, in turn, made merchants a rising class in Athenian political life and brought them into conflict with aristocrats. Class differences sharpened at every level, causing social unrest. The poor were often enslaved and sold to foreigners. Small landholders looked to aristocrats for protection in exchange for part of their agricultural production. But these payments eventually caused resentment. To lessen tensions, in 621 BCE, the lawgiver Draco established a written code of punishments to be handed out for various offenses. The code, which meant to curb increasing lawlessness and clan warfare, placed all power to render justice in the hands of the courts. It was notably harsh. A petty thief could be put to death, and lenders could enslave people who owed them money!

In 594 BCE, Athens appointed Solon as archon to reform the laws of Attica. Solon's reforms reduced the power of the aristocracy. Solon also wanted to place justice within the control of man, rather than in the hands of the gods. Solon was certain that *dike*, the principle of justice, could be interpreted without a god's intervention. When Solon left office, a power struggle followed, with the tyrant Peisistratus winning.

During Peisistratus's time in command, Athens became a major religious center. A temple to Athena, protectress of the city, was erected at the Acropolis in about 560 BCE. Fountains were also constructed, providing Athens with clear water. Eventually, Peisistratus's tyranny lost popularity because of a military defeat. Cleisthenes, a leader of a rival clan who had been living in exile, returned and drew up a plan of reform that allowed citizens to participate in government as equals. This was the first step in the development of direct democracy.

Peisistratus took control of Athens by force.

Darius I served as king of Persia from 522 to 486 BCE.

The Struggle for Supremacy: Classical Greece (500–323 BCE) and Hellenization (323–30 BCE)

At the beginning of the Classical period, Athens was the most influential polis. Its colonies in Asia Minor, however, suffered under the rule of Persian tyrants. By 499 BCE, some cities in Ionia, in present-day western Turkey, rose in revolt against Darius I, the Persian king. Both Athens and Eretria supported Ionia, and their combined forces burned down the Persian city of Sardis. Angered, the Persian army followed them back to Ionia and handed them a crushing defeat at Ephesus. Darius began to plot his revenge on Athens. In 490 BCE, his army invaded the Greek mainland, but Athens defeated the Persians at the Battle of Marathon.

Xerxes I was the son of Darius the Great.

The continued Persian threat convinced Athens and Sparta that they had more to gain by cooperating against their powerful opponent than by fighting one another. By the time Darius the Great's **successor**, Xerxes I, invaded the Greek mainland in 480 BCE, several of the city-states had allied themselves under the leadership of Sparta. The Persian army, estimated by some sources

successor (suhk-SES-ur) one who follows another in a position or sequence

The Battle of Thermopylae was one of the biggest of the Greco-Persian War.

maritime (MAR-i-time) having to do with the sea, ships, or navigation

to be 250,000 men strong, met 7,000 Greek soldiers at Thermopylae in eastern Greece. The Greeks fought valiantly for several days but eventually fell to the Persians. The mighty Greek fleet, however, turned back the invaders at Salamis, causing the Persian army to retreat.

The following year, the Greek allies trapped the Persian infantry at Plataea and decisively defeated it. The Greeks then went on the offensive against the Persian invaders. More than 150 city-states banded together to form the Delian League. The Greek allies continued to wage war against Persia for another thirty years, finally liberating the remaining colonies.

No sooner had the Greco-Persian War ended than the city-states returned to their pattern of fighting against each other. Threatened by the **maritime** superiority of Athens, in 431 BCE Sparta and its mainland allies, called the Peloponnesian League, repeatedly attacked Attica, the region that contained Athens. The assaults marked the beginning of the Peloponnesian War. Athens launched counterattacks against them using a clever strategy to overcome the superior might of Sparta and its allies on land. They would withdraw behind walls and use their stronger navy to disrupt Sparta's supply lines. The people of Attica flocked to Athens for protection, which led to overcrowding and widespread disease.

The Spartan military was known for its powerful ground forces.

By 426 BCE, disease had wiped out roughly one-third of the city's population. One of its victims was Athens's dynamic leader, Pericles. Called the "first citizen of Athens" by noted historian Thucydides, Pericles had strengthened Athens's position atop the Delian League, fostered the further development of democracy begun by the reforms of Cleisthenes, and instituted large-scale building projects.

The Athenian ruler Pericles fell victim to a deadly disease.

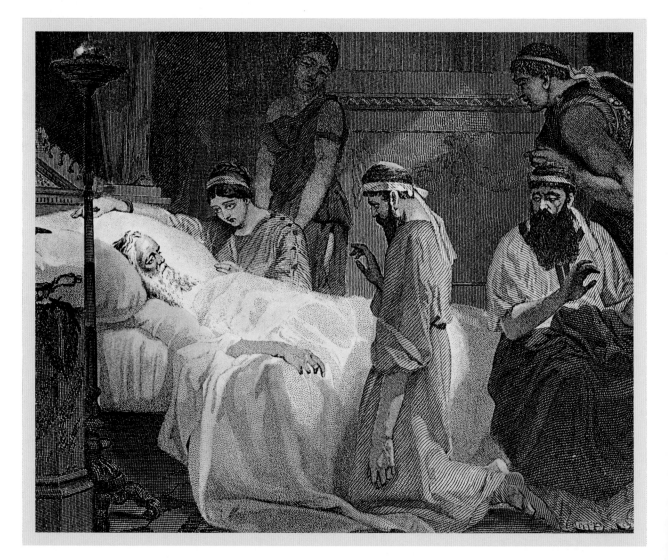

Weakened by disease and internal conflict, Athens failed in its attack on Sicily, the largest island in the Mediterranean. Sparta had worked behind the scenes to erode support among Athens's allies. In 405 BCE, Athens reached its breaking point. It had come to depend on a steady supply of imported grain from its colonies in Asia Minor. When the Spartan navy blocked ships carrying grain, Athens had the choice of starving or fighting against a stronger foe. Predictably, Athens lost the Battle of Aegospotami and accepted the harsh terms dictated by its foes. Athens turned over all of its overseas colonies, took down its protective city walls, and dismantled its fleet.

During the Battle of Aegospotami, Athens lost all but 20 of its 180 ships.

The assassination
of Philip II led to
Alexander the Great
assuming control of the
Macedonian Empire.

Sparta, however, was not powerful enough to control such a
widespread empire, and its supremacy was short-lived. Sensing
Sparta's weakness, Athens, Thebes, Argos, and Corinth waged war
against it. Persia's support of Sparta, however, kept Athens and
its allies from winning back their losses. But when Sparta moved
to extend control over Thebes in 371 BCE, Theban soldiers held
their ground.

Thebes was unable to maintain its control over Greece for long. In 362 BCE, Athens and Sparta joined forces to battle Thebes and its allies at Mantinea. All of the major city-states suffered heavy losses. As a result, Thebes and Athens offered little resistance to the military might of Philip II of Macedon, and he eventually gained control over all of Greece except Sparta. His son, Alexander (also known as Alexander the Great), defeated the Persian army and extended the Macedonian Empire and Greek influence as far east as the Indus River in India.

Alexander spread Greek language and culture throughout the Persian Empire. He founded twenty towns and cities bearing his name, the most famous being Alexandria in Egypt. Classical Athenian ideals in government, architecture, and education were combined with Persian standards to create a distinctive cultural mix called Hellenism. In the farthest reaches of Alexander's empire, aspects of Greek religion combined with the Hindu and Buddhist religions.

Greek influence also contributed to the development of Indian astronomy, which incorporated many classical Greek ideas. In return, Greek culture was influenced by Eastern art and philosophy. When most of Greece fell to the Romans after the Battle of Corinth in 146 BCE, this rich Hellenic culture influenced Roman intellectual life. Roman poets and playwrights adopted classical Greek styles, and many Roman leaders held the Greeks in high regard.

CHAPTER TWO

SOLVING THE RIDDLE OF SOCIAL ORDER

A ncient Greece's cultural contributions that have shaped much of our modern world would not have been possible without social order. Geographically, mountains and

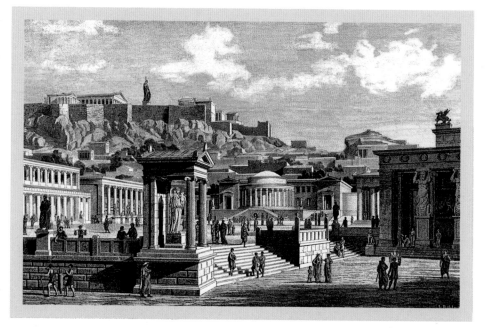

Each city-state had its own unique social structure.

rivers separate the many regions of Greece. Therefore, city-states developed independently from one another and created different institutions to meet the needs of that particular city-state. The complex mix of military and political events, as well as class struggle and clan warfare, often called for local solutions.

Sparta was one of the largest and most powerful Greek city-states.

City-states periodically found it in their common interest to help one another, especially in times of war against an invader. These experiences gave citizens of each polis a sense of a common Greek culture. Each citizen divided his loyalties between clan, polis, and country. Because Athens and Sparta were large and influential, it's helpful to compare and contrast them to better understand Greek government.

POLIS—THE COMMON ELEMENT

The concept of the polis can be traced to the Greek Dark Age. In about the eighth and seventh centuries BCE, large numbers of people were moving from the countryside to urban areas. Each city-state consisted of an urban center and a nearby region of scattered settlements. The sea, mountains, or an adjacent city-state often marked the boundaries of the polis. Cities served as centers for agricultural markets. Cities located on waterways served as centers for overseas trade. The people of each polis commonly came from a relatively small number of clans. Each polis had its own patron god, festivals, and sports competitions.

The polis was primarily a political unit. It began as an aristocratic system, with priests coming from established families. Eventually, the military began to assume a more central role in the affairs of the city-state. Women were excluded from political office. All cities probably had some institutions in common, such as an assembly of warriors, a council of elders, and judges elected annually.

No later than the sixth century BCE, city-states established a legal code. The code was usually, but not always, written. The laws of Solon were an important first step in the eventual development of Athenian democracy. In Sparta, the law code of Lycurgus established a fundamental reordering of society. It dissolved social tension among its citizens by making them all citizen-soldiers.

The Past Is Present
AN ENDURING STYLE

It was not until the middle of the eighteenth century, beginning in England, that direct study of the ruins of Athens became common. This led to a powerful revival of Greek architecture that swept across Europe and North America in the mid-nineteenth century. In a little more than a decade, almost two dozen Greek Revival churches

were constructed in London. Other Greek Revival gems in England include London's Covent Garden, the British Museum, and the National Gallery (above). In North America, Thomas Jefferson was especially influential in bringing the Greek Revival

to the United States. Jefferson's home, Monticello (left), and the University of Virginia campus are prime examples of the Greek Revival's influence on him. As a result of his influence, thousands of Greek Revival structures were constructed, and still stand, in small towns and cities throughout the United States.

Councils and assemblies met to determine local government issues.

Within a century, city-states found it necessary to define more precisely the concept of what constituted a citizen. The polis had to determine how a citizen would differ from a noncitizen in terms of rights and responsibilities. Groups outside of the citizen class were also sharply defined. Citizens were expected to participate as equals in all matters of politics and the law. Before long, aristocratic citizens used their wealth to steer the affairs of state. Class struggle between rich and poor citizens became common. This was most noticeable in the outposts of Magna Graecia, or the Greek colonies, where wealthy landholders with more education held most of the political power.

Helots had little chance to increase their social standing.

The *Politeia*: Sparta's Constitution

After Sparta achieved victory in the Messenian War, the helots who remained in Sparta posed a problem for the city-state. Helots were not technically slaves, but they were not free and were not citizens. A helot's children would themselves be helots for life unless they could accumulate enough wealth to buy their freedom. Occasionally, they would be freed. Some helots owned property. Vastly outnumbering citizens, helots presented an ongoing threat of rebellion. It was in Sparta's best interests to require military training and service from each citizen. This social revolution helped decrease class tensions throughout the polis and fostered self-sufficiency.

Spartan citizens were those who succeeded in the state's rigorous military training and education, called the *agoge*. Not everyone could receive this education. Generally, only young men whose ancestors were among Sparta's founders, the Spartiates, qualified. Sometimes, the sons of important leaders from other city-states would be accepted into the agoge. Spartiate families occasionally adopted helots and paid their tuition in the agoge. In this way, helots could escape their lives of servitude and become citizens if they met the challenges of the agoge.

Sparta's government balanced political power between kings, aristocratic institutions, and democratic elements. Two kings, descendants of the Eurypontid and Agiad families, ruled the polis. They possessed roughly equal power. Kings held religious roles and oversaw **rituals** and sacrifices. They also had limited legal power and were military leaders.

Power gradually passed from the hands of Sparta's two kings and became centered in more democratic institutions. A board of five ephors, or judges, was elected annually. Ephors could never

rituals (RICH-oo-uhlz) acts or series of acts that are always performed in the same way, usually as part of a religious or social ceremony

Spartan kings joined their troops in battle.

be reelected. They had broad judicial and executive powers, were actively involved in maintaining a disciplined society, and made decisions by majority rule. Ephors presided over the agoge and called the citizen assembly, or *ekklesia*, to order. They had the power to declare war. Ephors could also bring incompetent or corrupt officials to justice. They exercised some supervisory power over Sparta's two hereditary kings as well. Unlike Sparta's dual monarchy, all citizens could in theory be elected ephors. The office continued until the third century CE, when it began to gradually disappear.

In Sparta, full citizens over the age of thirty met on the seventh day of each month in the ekklesia. The ekklesia's powers were considerable. It sometimes met at the same time as the *gerousia*, a council of twenty-eight elders over the age of sixty. When a joint meeting was presided over by an ephor, the ekklesia was empowered to sign

The Spartan ekklesia had the power to declare war against other city-states.

Spartan kings held a great deal of power, but were not the sole voice of government.

The Athenian ekklesia held its meetings on a hill called the Pnyx.

treaties, declare war, free helots, appoint infantry commanders, and elect ephors. Though the ekklesia was open to all Spartiate males over the age of thirty, it only gradually became more democratic. Aristocrats could speak and make proposals, but ordinary citizens were barred from doing the same. If citizens approved of a measure, they might applaud or shout in agreement. If they disapproved, the proposal was met with silence.

Members of the gerousia, drawn from Sparta's elite, were appointed for life by shouts of approval before the ekklesia. The gerousia ultimately controlled which matters would be considered by the ekklesia. It interpreted laws and presided over major criminal trials. The gerousia changed during the later Hellenistic and Roman periods. Then, only 23 men were appointed for a period of one year, and Spartiates became eligible after age forty. Spartan government was remarkable for coherently blending elements of monarchy and democracy while dissolving many class-based distinctions between citizens.

ATHENIAN DEMOCRACY

From about 508 to 321 BCE, the polis of Athens had direct democracy, which was different in many ways from the representative democracy of the United States. In a direct democracy, the people themselves, rather than elected representatives, vote on policies and laws. The word *democracy* comes from the Greek word *demokratia*, meaning "the rule of the people." Then, as now, democracy was tied up with the concept of liberty. It implied "freedom"—not only to take part in the political institutions of Athens, especially citizen assemblies, but also the freedom to live life as one pleased and to speak one's mind.

In classical Athens, only Athenian men had political rights. Slaves, women, and foreigners could not participate in citizen assemblies. At age eighteen, an Athenian male was listed in his father's deme, a local political unit. Attica consisted of 139 of these local units. Young men served the next two years in Athens's military. When they reached the age of twenty, they could take part in the ekklesia. They could not, however, take part in all aspects of Athenian democracy until age thirty. In the fourth century BCE, the population of Attica was about 260,000. Of those, about thirty thousand were citizens with full political rights.

Meetings of the ekklesia were usually attended by at least five thousand citizens. Forty meetings were held each year. Politically active citizens made speeches, and votes on matters before the

Large groups of people met at the Agora to hold trials and discuss important issues.

assembly were taken by a show of hands. Citizens in the ekklesia could elect military judges, appoint legislators, or name judges to hear a trial. Although the ekklesia could render decisions on matters of foreign policy or decrees affecting the polis, it could not make law. Instead, once each year, full citizens selected a group from among themselves to serve for that year both as judges and legislators. When laws were enacted, the ekklesia drew lots and appointed one thousand of themselves as legislators for that day only. Next, laws and amendments to the law code established by Solon were debated. At the conclusion of the debate, legislators made a decision regarding the law.

The courts, or *dikasteria*, met about two hundred days each year. On days when the court was in session, some of the six thousand citizens who volunteered or were drawn by lot to serve would come to the Agora, Athens's gathering place. Several courts for the day would be appointed from gathered citizens. Courts hearing matters involving disputes between citizens would usually have either two hundred or four hundred citizen judges. Trials considering constitutional issues or charges against corrupt leaders were usually heard by panels of about five hundred people. Judges presided over each of the appointed courts, whose sessions often lasted nine hours. In order to be a judge, a citizen had to be over thirty years of age and had to seek the appointment. The ekklesia chose about one hundred of them. An additional eleven hundred were chosen by drawing lots. Five hundred of these were appointed councilors, and the remainder were appointed other judges.

Most judges served a one-year term and could never serve again. Special care was taken in grouping judges for specific purposes. Most often, ten were grouped, one coming from each tribe, in an effort to ensure all groups and regions of Attica were represented. Judges presided over the courts and saw that the decisions rendered were faithfully executed. The boule, a council of five hundred, was far more influential in steering the daily affairs of state. Membership was open to all citizens except *thetes*, hired laborers whose lands produced few crops. Although they could participate in the assembly, the boule was closed to them.

The boule decided what issues would be placed before the ekklesia for its consideration. It gradually acquired administrative power over the polis's finances and public buildings, as well as responsibility for maintaining Athens's navy and infantry. The boule eventually assumed judicial powers as well. Historians have concluded that the boule was the part of government most essential for coordinating the activities of Athenian democracy. In times of war, however, it might have been surpassed by the *strategoi*, Athens's ten elected generals.

Lycurgus believed that all citizens should be required to serve in the military.

Participation in Athenian democracy, especially the courts, could be very time-consuming. This created a conflict for poorer citizens. Fearing that participation in Athens's government institutions placed too great a financial burden on ordinary citizens, Pericles began to pay those participating in the boule and popular courts. Late in the fourth century BCE, new positions were introduced, including a minister of finance. However, after the Macedonian conquest, democracy was largely suspended, and Athens was ruled by a small group of aristocrats.

Both Athenian democracy and Sparta's mixed system addressed common social realities. In Sparta, the outcome of the first Messenian War provided the Spartans an opportunity to relieve class tensions. Lycurgus was free to institute a system requiring compulsory military service of each citizen. All men, regardless of class, had the same duties to the state.

In Athens, the reforms of Cleisthenes lent support to democratic principles and institutions. Men of different social and economic classes, or from different clans, were brought together by the creation of 139 demes throughout Attica. The reordering broke down many of the existing distinctions based on clan and family loyalties, subordinating both to the new democratic state and its institutions. Those institutions provided opportunities for ordinary citizens to participate in the day-to-day workings of government. The effect, as in Sparta, was the creation of a society where men worked, more than ever before, toward the same ends.

Lycurgus was responsible for many changes to Spartan law.

CHAPTER THREE

THE FORCES THAT SHAPED ANCIENT GREECE

In hindsight, it seems that ancient Greece was destined, or fated, to develop as it did. Its mountains, lakes, and rivers encouraged the formation of numerous, isolated city-states. Its long coastline fostered colonization and overseas trade. Its relative lack of farmable land, and the irregular distribution of it, guaranteed periodic food shortages. These conditions brought one polis into conflict with another. Greece's variety of climates helped establish local cultures and patterns of trade, which in turn spread cultural practices.

A LAND OF MOUNTAINS, RIVERS, AND LAKES

Ancient Greece was located on the southernmost part of the Balkan Peninsula. One major mountain range, the Pindus of northern Greece, is approximately 100 miles (161 kilometers) long. Its highest peak is Mount Smolikas, Greece's second-highest mountain, at more than 8,650 feet (2,636 m). The highest peak

in Greece is Mount Olympus, on the border of Macedonia and Thessaly, at 9,570 feet (2,917 m). For the ancients, Olympus was at the northernmost border of Greece. People then believed that Olympus was the home of Zeus and the other gods.

Mountains comprised about three-quarters of the area of ancient Greece. They formed distinct geographical boundaries between mainland Greece's plains, wetlands, hillsides, fertile plateaus, and coastal regions. The mountains, steep and rocky, could not be cultivated, but occasionally hillsides set on softer rocks could be. The Greeks prized the country's fertile plains, and city-states occasionally fought for control of them.

Mount Olympus was a site of great importance in the ancient Greek religion.

The Past Is Present
"I SWEAR BY APOLLO..."

Hippocrates (ca. 460–ca. 370 BCE) was a Greek physician, often referred to as the father of Western medicine. He founded the Hippocratic school of medicine, which established medicine as a study distinctly different from other notable Greek disciplines such as philosophy and the practice of rituals. The *Hippocratic Corpus* is his most notable work, a collection of textbooks, philosophical essays, and notes on different subjects in medicine. His most enduring contribution, which is still in use today, is the Hippocratic oath. It is an oath, or promise, taken by doctors and other health care professionals to practice medicine ethically. The original text requiring that a new physician swear upon several gods has been changed. But the almost 2,500-year-old tradition of treating disease and respecting the sick remains unchanged to this day.

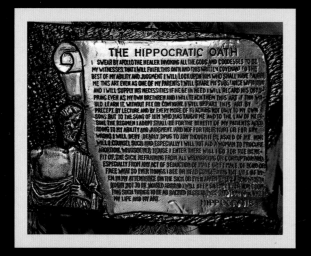

MOUNTAINS

Mountains were densely covered with forests of beech, oak, and pine trees in the north and cypress trees on Crete. The economic success of city-states depended, in part, on having access to a variety of resources. Both Attica and Sparta were large and had many resources. Yet Athens could not always grow enough barley, which was more important than wheat in the Classical Age. Athens often imported timber, too.

In ancient times, rivers were seen as gods or ancestors of heroes. During battles, sacrifices were commonly offered to rivers. Beyond their cultural and religious significance, rivers were navigated for trade

City-states used waterways to trade goods with one another.

The crews of trading ships avoided shallow waters by carrying their ships across the Isthmus of Corinth.

and might serve as a boundary between a city-state and its neighbors. The largest rivers of Greece—including Pineios, Acheloos, Aliakmon, Arachthos, and Kalamas—originate in the Pindus Mountains. Eurotas and Alfios originate in the Taygetos Mountains on the Peloponnese Peninsula in southern Greece.

ISLANDS AND SEA

The sea was also important to life in ancient Greece. Mainland Greece is bordered on the west by the Ionian Sea, on the south by the Mediterranean Sea, and on the east by the Aegean Sea. Coastal city-states with good harbors, such as Athens and its port Piraeus, were able to prosper. Maritime trade increased the

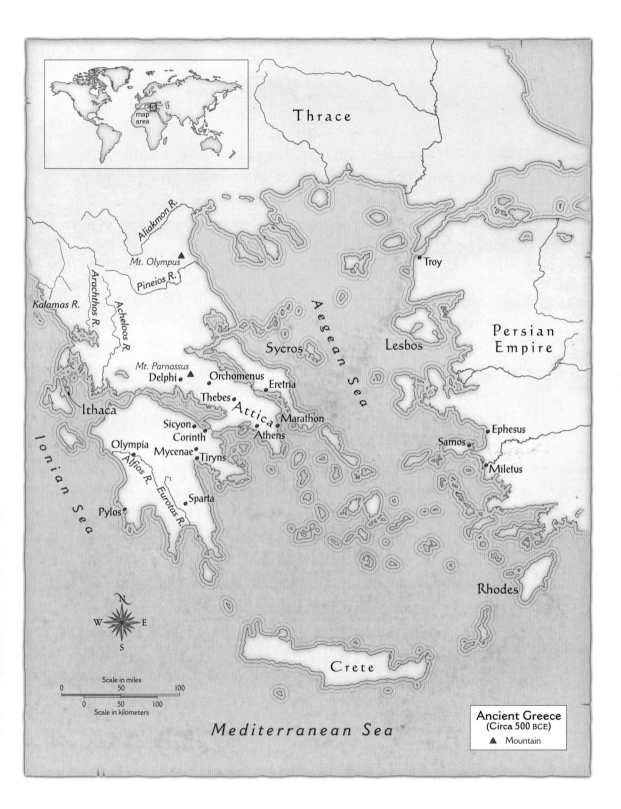

Thrace

Aliakmon R.

Mt. Olympus ▲

Pineios R.

Kalamas R.

Arachthos R.

Acheloos R.

Troy

Persian Empire

Aegean Sea

Lesbos

Sycros

Mt. Parnassus ▲
Delphi
Orchomenus
Eretria
Thebes
Attica
Marathon

Ithaca

Sicyon
Corinth
Athens

Olympia
Mycenae
Tiryns

Samos
Ephesus

Miletus

Alfios R.

Eurotas R.

Sparta

Pylos

Ionian Sea

Rhodes

N
W   E
S

Crete

Scale in miles
0   50   100

0   50   100
Scale in kilometers

Mediterranean Sea

Ancient Greece
(Circa 500 BCE)
▲ Mountain

isthmus (IS-muhs) a narrow strip of land that lies between two bodies of water and connects two larger landmasses

amount of resources available to a city-state. As a result, the population and prosperity of Athens grew relatively quickly.

Because ships often followed the coastline when sailing from one part of Greece to another, and because the coastline was so long, trade could be very slow. In addition, sailing around the Peloponnese was dangerous. Ships frequently sank in shallow coastal waters, especially at Cape Malea with its strong winds. To minimize the risks of this water route, the Greeks built the Diolkos, a paved trackway, across the **Isthmus** of Corinth around 600 BCE. There, ships were transported overland.

The importance—and dangers—of maritime travel continued to be an inspiration for Greek innovation. The three-masted ship, a more stable sailing vessel, appeared by the middle of the third century BCE. This innovation was followed by the construction of the lighthouse at Alexandria, Egypt.

Safer and faster travel by water expanded Greece's trade with its colonies. Minoan civilization began on Crete, the largest of the islands of ancient Greece. Euboea, the second-largest island and home of Eretria and Chalcis, became an active commercial center. By 750 BCE, the Greeks were faced with a rapidly growing population and limited farmable land. To solve the problem, the Greeks began looking to colonize the Mediterranean. They established colonies on the eastern coast of the Black Sea, at Massalia (now Marseille, France's second-largest city), and in eastern Libya. They also established outposts on Sicily and along the southern coast of the Italian Peninsula in Apulia and Calabria.

The outposts created by Greek colonization were politically independent of their polis. Yet colonization spread Greek culture, in particular its music, religion, and architecture, to Italy. Most

The Alexandria lighthouse was one of the Seven Wonders of the Ancient World.

importantly, it brought the Greek alphabet, which was ultimately transformed into the Roman alphabet. A number of Greece's colonies in Italy—including Naples, Syracuse, Tarentum, and Elea—became influential trade and intellectual centers.

Two Seasons, Many Climates

The development of ancient Greece was also shaped by its climate. There were two seasons: a winter that was wet and cool, and a dry, hot summer. From one year to another, there were occasionally large changes in the amount of rainfall. **Famine** was common as farmers struggled to eke out large enough harvests to support a growing population.

famine (FAM-in) a serious lack of food in a geographic area

Droughts sometimes left ancient Greek farmers unable to produce enough food.

drought (DROUT) a long period without rain

Many factors affect local climate. One of the most important is wind direction. Because Greece is so mountainous, westerly winds dump more rain on the western side of its mountain ranges and leave areas to the east relatively dry. As a result, Attica and Euboea were drier than Epirus and Aetolia, and were more prone to **drought** and famine. Both Attica and Euboea played major roles in the wave of colonization between 750 and 500 BCE. Attica, with a population of three hundred thousand by the fifth century BCE, depended heavily on imports of wheat and barley grown overseas in western Asia Minor.

Altitude played an important role in climate and agricultural production. In addition, regions near the sea experienced less seasonal variation in temperature. With fertile soils, they could hope for two growing seasons. Hardy strains of wheat, which grew better in colder temperatures, were imported from the north shores of the Black Sea. Farmers sometimes used a simple wooden plow to break the soil. If they had very little land, they used a spade and a hoe.

Greece's mountainous terrain, closeness to the seas, and winds combined to determine its agricultural choices and its patterns of territorial expansion and trade. Because it lies at the point where Europe, Asia, and Africa meet, it also had unlimited opportunities for trade. This location, however, also guaranteed that ancient Greece would often be at war.

Olives were an important crop in some parts of Greece.

CHAPTER FOUR

LIVES OF SIMPLICITY AND BALANCE

E veryday life in Greece varied among city-states and was different for men and women. Social roles were clearly defined at each stage of life and for each social class in every polis. Religious beliefs, music, games, and festivals were similar from one

The ancient Greeks celebrated a variety of holidays and festivals.

polis to the next. It is possible, therefore, to examine the elements of Greek daily life that were held in common and to see the ways particular city-states differed from that pattern.

Central courtyards were often centers of activity.

GREEK HOUSES

By the Classical and Hellenistic Ages, Greek houses were much the same everywhere. Houses were made of mudbrick on a stone foundation. They had few windows, and those they did have were small. Visitors entered a doorway on the street, walking through a short passageway directly into a small, rectangular courtyard.

Rooms of the house were arranged around the central courtyard. The interior walls of those rooms were plastered and painted in plain colors, usually white or red. Floors were formed by adding lime, chalk, and a variety of other substances to the earth, then beating down the mixture to create a strong, compact surface. A second floor was reached by ladder, as staircases were uncommon in private homes. There were two types of roofs: pitched and flat. The pitched style was more common in areas with higher rainfall, and the flat roof was used in dry climates. Roofs were made of brush and clay tiles.

Pitched roofs prevented rainwater from pooling on top of ancient Greek homes.

The Past Is Present
LET THE GAMES BEGIN!

The oldest and most prominent of the Panhellenic festivals were the ancient Olympic Games in the Elis region of southern Greece. The games helped to forge a common Greek identity and emphasized the greatness of human achievement dedicated to a higher purpose. The first games were held in 776 BCE. They reached their peak in the sixth and fifth centuries BCE, but declined in importance as the Romans gained power and influence in Greece. The games were officially ended in 393 CE, and were not held again until the late nineteenth century.

Today, the competitions are held every two years, with Summer and Winter Olympic Games alternating. Thousands of athletes from more than 200 nations participate in a variety of sporting events. In 2008, 4.7 billion television viewers—70 percent of the world's population—tuned in to watch the Summer Olympics held in Beijing, China. The 2012 Summer Olympics were held in London, England. The 2014 Winter Olympics will be held in Sochi in the Russian Federation, and the 2016 Summer Olympics will be held in Rio de Janeiro, Brazil.

symposium (sim-PO-zee-um) a party with wine, music, and conversation

Only men were allowed to attend symposia.

The main living room was often quite large and faced south, making it warmer in winter. Most rooms were decorated simply. The *andron*, or the room for men, was an exception. Its floor was usually cement and raised on each side, with a lower rectangle in the middle. Several dining couches, cushions, and low tables were placed along the sides of the andron to accommodate male guests during a **symposium**. Symposia provided aristocratic men an opportunity to bond with one another. They drank wine served by slave boys, listened to music, and enjoyed poetry readings. The parties, which excluded females, frequently spilled out onto the street.

Ancient Greek families often had workshops where they could practice their crafts.

Though women were not permitted in the andron, the house was considered their domain. Women were the economic supervisors of the home, responsible for cloth production and household management. To avoid male visitors, they frequently kept to parts of the house where men were unlikely to go, such as the upstairs women's room, called the *gynaikon*. There, they entertained friends or tended to their children while spinning and weaving.

Often, a room directly off the courtyard was set aside for crafts. If the family worked in gold, for example, their tools and workbenches would be there. This room often had a door directly on the street because the home was also the place where a family worked

Ancient Greek fashion was based around loose, draping clothing.

and sold their goods. The courtyard sometimes contained larger tools and very often had a well or reservoir for collecting rainwater. The basic design of the Greek house was the same everywhere, whether in cities or in the country. Some houses had towers used for storage. Generally, all private homes were very modest in size and furnishings. Beginning in the fourth century BCE, Greeks occasionally built much larger homes with two courtyards.

Simple Attire

The simple elegance of the Greeks' homes was matched by their dress. Most often, clothes were made of wool, although linen was occasionally used for tunics. Aristocratic women sometimes wore brightly decorated silk. All weaving was done on traditional looms. Occasionally, more complex patterns were tapestry woven. Purple was a special, expensive dye, made from sea snails. When garments were dyed, care was taken to apply purple in geometric patterns.

Freeborn citizens wore the himation, a rectangular, loose cloak without sleeves, measuring 6 feet x 9 feet (1.8 x 2.7 m) and pinned at the shoulder. These were often used as blankets at night. Some other garments, such as tunics, were worn instead of the himation. They were often bleached white, with a decorated, colorful hem. Women wore the peplos, a garment made from a square piece of cloth folded over and pinned at both shoulders. The peplos was worn in the countryside and during cool weather. Women wore linen tunics under the wool, and men wore linen loincloths.

Both men and women wore leather shoes or sandals. Women wore a hairnet, the *sakkos*, and stretchy socks called *sokkoi*. Women adorned themselves with makeup, had their hair beautifully styled, and wore elaborate jewelry.

Pleasures of Daily Life

Dance, music, theater, festivals, and games were important parts of daily life in Greece. Greek dance was believed to be a gift from the gods to mankind. Specific dances were associated with different types of theater. For example, the bawdy *kordax* was performed in comedies, and the somber *emmelia* was performed in tragedies. Each dance served to reinforce the tone of the play. In Greece's colonies, plays gently mocking the dances of religious festivals became popular. Professional dancers, often slaves, performed at symposia in the androns of aristocratic households. People danced to celebrate victory in battle. They also danced at weddings and funerals.

Some dances became famous, like the *partheneion* of Greek maidens, which was accompanied with song and performed as part of religious rites on joyous occasions. Another, the *askoliasmos*, was performed on greased wineskins and provided much comic amusement. Sometimes, dances were mingled with the worship of a specific god, such as the frenzied *oreibasia* of women honoring Dionysus.

Music and dance together were considered essential to celebration. Music, too, was seen as a divine gift to humanity and essential to communication with the gods. All Greeks, regardless of social class, danced, sang, and played musical instruments. In Greek theater, the absence of music often implied a curse or warned of death or war. At weddings and funerals, the *kithara*, or box lyre, was always played. Music created a sense of community. The polis was much more than a city of walls and buildings: it was a social grouping united by common cultural experiences.

At Panhellenic festivals, instrumentalists and choruses competed against one another, paralleling the fierce athletic

competitions. These festivals brought together participants from all corners of the Greek realm, mainland and colonies. The events, which took place in a four-year cycle, contributed greatly to the Greek sense of identity and shared experience. Because of their competitive nature, the festivals advanced the art of music in Greece. By bringing together musicians and citizens from Greece's city-states and colonies, the festivals helped to forge the sense of a shared culture among the people. Similar local and regional festivals further reinforced a sense of community.

The ancient Greeks often amused themselves by going to see theater performances.

Footraces were a staple of the ancient Greek Olympics.

These festivals, founded to honor deities or local heroes, grew in size and cultural importance. The Pythian, Nemean, Isthmian, and Olympic Games formed a four-year cycle of sports festivals, though only the last one has had an enduring popularity. The Olympic Games, oldest of the four, began in 776 BCE to honor Zeus. They were held near the polis of Elis in the western Peloponnese. Participation was limited to free men who spoke Greek. Women and slaves were excluded from athletic events.

In their early years, the ancient Olympic Games featured only footraces. One of the most popular and challenging was the *hoplitodromos*. Less than 0.5 mile in length (0.8 km), it was a sprint in full armor, including shield and helmet. Frequently, runners collapsed under the strain, requiring their competitors to leap over them. Other events were added, including boxing, wrestling, discus and javelin throwing, long jumping, and the *pankration*, a bloody event much like mixed martial arts with few rules. At Zeus's temple in Olympia, victors were awarded the *kotinos*, a wreath made from wild olive leaves, which were sacred to Zeus.

Although athletic games were undoubtedly the most popular competitions, the Greeks also sponsored contests in music and poetry. There were contests for playwrights and chariot racers, and even drinking contests. Each celebrated a distinctive aspect of Greek culture and helped to spread it.

WORLDS WITHIN THE WORLD

Education was the cornerstone of Greek society. It implied broad cultural training rather than academic schooling alone. In the Archaic Age, as well as the early Classical, the works of poets were

Wrestling was a popular event at the Olympic Games.

used to help educate students. Children learned by reciting poetry or participating in festivals. There is no evidence of schools before about 500 BCE. The earliest schools taught elementary skills and were largely for the wealthy, focusing on gymnastics and music.

Sparta designed its educational system with the goal of enhancing the polis's military might. At age seven, boys left their families and lived in barracks. Though physical education was the top priority, Sparta's children were also trained in music and learned to read and write. Girls were educated in gymnastics, dance, and music. When boys reached the age of twelve, they

Spartan boys exercised and learned the art of combat.

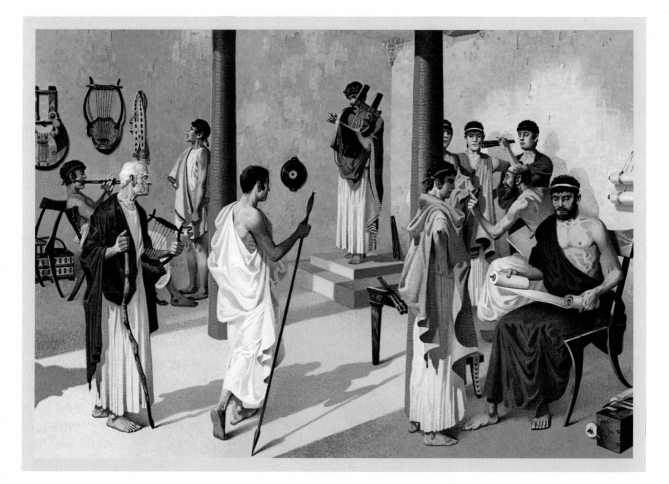

were placed under the supervision of a **mentor**. At age eighteen, they completed rigorous military training. They remained in active military service until they were thirty and in active reserve until sixty. In this way, Spartan men learned loyalty to their polis and to their fellow infantrymen.

In Athens, early education was designed with somewhat different priorities. There, education was comprised of three elements, which were taught in different schools. Physical education, which included gymnastics and fitness, was taught by the *paidotribes*. Children learned music and poetry from the *kitharistes*, and they learned reading, writing, arithmetic, and literature from the

Athenian students learned about a wide variety of subjects, including math and philosophy.

mentor (MEHN-tor) a wise and trusted adviser

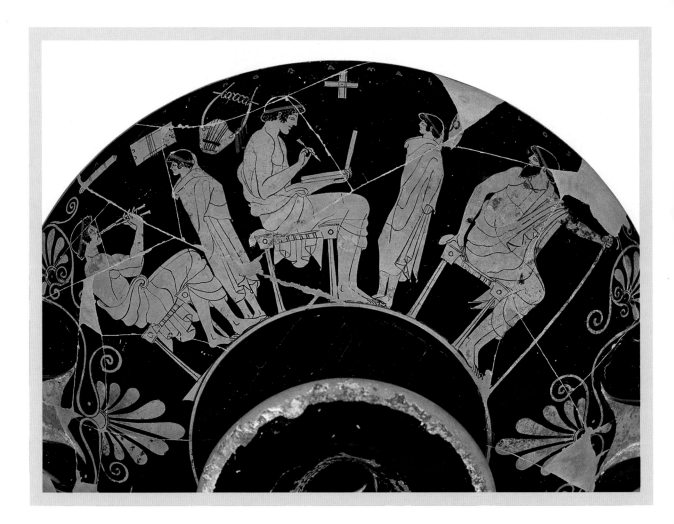

The artwork on this vase illustrates the Athenian commitment to education.

grammatistes. At first, the families of students paid for this education, which involved a teacher and student in a private setting. Parents could decide which schools their children would attend. Children were taken to and from lessons by slaves, and were beaten by teachers with canes if they misbehaved. Once the reforms of Solon and Cleisthenes set Attica on the path to democracy, Athens instituted group schooling to educate citizens for the new state.

By the end of the fifth century BCE, education began to take on a more important role. The flourishing of classical philosophy provided opportunities for more advanced study at schools devoted to science, mathematics, medicine, and philosophy. Higher education also aimed to provide training in morals and political skills. As a result, the study of poetry became less important as educators stressed writing and the logical structure of language. The Hellenistic Age replaced education's aristocratic leanings with a new emphasis on the ordinary citizen.

BOUND AND FREE

Helots had a totally different day-to-day experience. Bound to the land, they labored to produce the agricultural products for Sparta. They grew the wheat and barley used to make Sparta's porridge and bread. They cultivated onions, garlic, lettuce, leeks, celery, and cucumbers. Plants growing in the wild supplemented these foods. Figs, pears, and grapes were also grown. Despite their servitude, helots were given the freedoms of family life, with the slim chance of one day being free. Yet citizens could also kill helots without fear of punishment.

In city-states with few slaves, ordinary citizens cultivated their own food. As a result, citizens worked from dawn to dusk at planting and harvest times. At harvest time, political service occasionally came into conflict with the responsibilities of agricultural life. Besides farming, Greeks labored at a number of occupations. Men were carpenters and masons, shepherds and shipwrights, miners and smiths, merchants and jewelers. Others were musicians, painters, sculptors, or philosophers. A few were scientists, historians, astronomers, or actors. Women were spinners and weavers of linen and wool. They were bakers and seamstresses. They also performed the hard work of grinding grain by hand with stones. Some were priestesses, and others were dancers.

CHAPTER FIVE

THE GLORY OF ANCIENT GREECE

The development of ancient Greek civilization was tied to its religious beliefs, its literature and art, its technological and scientific advances, and its cultural practices. Religion was inseparable from Greek culture. From the beginning, religion was a shared public experience. It was, along with political life, the foundation of social structure.

Some of the Greek deities originated and evolved from earlier deities of other civilizations. Zeus most likely evolved from a sky god of eastern Europe and central Asia. Other deities bear a striking resemblance to gods and goddesses in Indian religion. Mount Olympus, the traditional home of the gods, shares some similarities with the ancient World Tree of the East. Other aspects of Greek belief arose from Mycenaean religion. Archaeologists believe that in making Poseidon their main deity, Mycenaeans may have been influenced by the earlier Minoan religion.

Poseidon was celebrated as the god of water, horses, and earthquakes.

The Past Is Present
MODERN-DAY MYTHOLOGY

The ancient Greeks expressed their ideologies in many ways, but perhaps none is as rich as that of their mythology, much of which has endured to this day. Some myths date back to before 1600 BCE, when the Minoan civilization flourished on Crete. In their earliest forms, myths were passed down orally from generation to generation, but in later centuries they were fashioned into literature and plays. The subject of most Greek myths is the hero, who must overcome enormous challenges to achieve his goal—often in a battle between good and evil. The hero frequently possesses superhuman, almost godlike, powers, such as great strength. The tradition of the Greek hero is seen in today's comic book superheroes, who use their amazing powers to fight evil against insurmountable obstacles. Comics and Greek myths share another function: teaching moral lessons about the nature of the world.

The Greeks practiced **polytheism**, a form of religion that believes in more than one god. Gods and goddesses each ruled over a particular aspect of nature. No god or goddess was all-powerful, but each was supreme in one aspect of nature. Zeus ruled over lightning and thunder. Poseidon ruled the seas and earthquakes. Helios ruled the sun. Some presided over mysterious realms: Hades ruled the Underworld and was the god of the dead, and Aphrodite controlled love. The Greek gods had human character weaknesses, but unlike humans they were immortal.

City-states were often under the protection of a particular deity. Aphrodite was protectress of Corinth. Athena was central to daily life and worship in Athens. Zeus was worshipped at Olympia. Gods and goddesses became symbolic of city-states. When Homer wrote of war between the gods in *The Iliad*, he was referring to the endless warfare between city-states of Greece.

Festivals, ceremonial practices, and sacrifices were of central importance in Greek culture. Festivals brought citizens together, promoting competition in athletics and the arts. Some were local and helped to promote a sense of community for a polis. Others, like the Panhellenic festivals, served a similar function for all of Greece.

polytheism (POL-ee-thee-iz-uhm) belief in more than one god

Aphrodite was the goddess of love and beauty.

Animals such as oxen were sacrificed as offerings to the gods.

Each of these festivals, including the four in the Panhellenic cycle, was dedicated to a deity. Zeus was honored at both the Olympic and Nemean Games, Apollo at the Pythian Games, and Poseidon at the Isthmian Games. The Games were considered an offering to the gods and also an embodiment of Greek cultural ideals.

Because festivals often combined athletics and arts in equal proportions, they promoted the ideal of a balanced mind and body in Greek life. Moderation lay at the core of Greek moral thought. To eat or drink in excess was wrong. To show excessive pride was also wrong and was considered a shameful act.

Ceremonies and animal sacrifices were important parts of Greek religion and cultural life. Animal sacrifices played several roles. The sacrificed animal was an offering to a deity. After the sacrifice, meat was cooked over a fire and shared among those present. This meal served to bond the religious community, just as the sacrifice had bonded the community to its deity. Sacrifices of sheep and goats were especially common. Homer's *Iliad* and *The Odyssey*, both epic poems, depict warriors sacrificing animals to gods at banquets, suggesting that the gods were honored guests present at those feasts.

Bloodless sacrifices were also common. Cakes, ritual dishes of fruits and grains, and wine were common offerings. At symposia, wine was mixed with water and offered to the deities. Another type of ritual was for the purpose of purification. The Greeks believed that the problems experienced by a polis were because of spiritual

Goats were often used in ceremonies to rid a polis of its problems.

pollution and that the pollution could be removed ritually. The pollution was "placed" on an animal, called the scapegoat, which was then sacrificed. Occasionally, humans were made scapegoats and were banished from the community. Yet another class of ritual, initiation rituals, focused on transitions from one life stage to another. These transitions required the blessing and protection of the gods.

Votive offerings were a common part of Greek culture. In a votive offering, a person placed an object or several objects in a sacred place as a gift to the gods. The Greeks built temples to store their votives, which were often statue likenesses of the god. Temples also served an important worldly purpose: the grandest in each city-state was a point of community pride.

Literature, Philosophy, and the Theater

Literature, especially the epic poetry of Homer, played a central role in Greek culture. Dating to the second half of the eighth century BCE, *The Iliad* and *The Odyssey* reflect the Greeks' fascination with the Mediterranean world during the age of colonization. The two works are also steeped in the cult of heroes and deities. Yet they are not mere histories. Homer's *Iliad*, set in the tenth year of the mythical Trojan War, focuses on only four days of battle. It depicts the horrors of war, showing that women and children suffer and that men die needlessly.

The central heroes of *The Iliad* were great warriors, but Homer also emphasized their humanity. The Greek hero Achilles kills many men in battle, but he mourns the loss of his friend Patroclus. Achilles gets his revenge, but later mourns the senselessness of war.

Homer's epics were studied in the schools of Archaic and Classical Greece. Students learned the importance of honoring

kinsmen and friends, but they also learned about the heartache of war. They came to understand that the gods communicated with them, walked among them, and took an interest in their daily affairs.

By the fifth century BCE, theater had gained importance. Greek tragedy, like the epic poetry of Homer, was founded on heroic myth. Tragedies reflected contemporary concerns and practices. Sophocles's tragedy *Oedipus Tyrannus*, for example, emphasizes the conflict of city and family, and examines the practice of scapegoating. Greek tragedy frequently examined debates originating in the ekklesia, shedding new light on them. Tragedies often helped citizens connect their daily lives with larger philosophical questions.

Ancient Greek theaters, such as the one at Epidauros, were built to hold huge crowds of spectators.

The Athenian philosopher Plato believed good government would only be possible if philosophers became kings or if kings studied philosophy. Plato founded Athens's influential Academy based on the principles of his philosophy. Plato's writings all take the form of dialogues in which characters discuss moral and philosophical problems. Instead of presenting a single viewpoint that he expected his readers to adopt, Plato always forced them to think for themselves and come to their own conclusions.

Plato made fundamental contributions to political thought as well. In his *Republic*, he put forward the idea that the individual soul and the polis are similar in structure. Each has three parts. The soul is composed of reason, spirit, and desire. The state is composed of rulers, their assistants, and ordinary citizens. For citizens and rulers alike, justice comes from harmonizing their interests with the common interest of the polis. Similarly, the individual must work to harmonize reason, spirit, and desire; justice derives from the rule of reason. Plato also made interesting contributions to the understanding of the afterlife, including rebirth, that were at odds with traditional classical religious beliefs.

The flowering of Greek philosophy had a profound effect on education. By the fourth century BCE, advanced students could further their education at one of several schools: Plato's Academy, Aristotle's Lyceum, or Isocrates's school of **rhetoric**. Others might study privately with educators who taught rhetoric and political virtue.

ANCIENT GREEK SCIENCE AND TECHNOLOGY

Greek science at first concerned itself with practical matters. In his *Works and Days*, Hesiod wrote about a calendar that would be useful to farmers, based on seasonal patterns of stars. Though Greek

Plato is considered one of the greatest thinkers of ancient Greece.

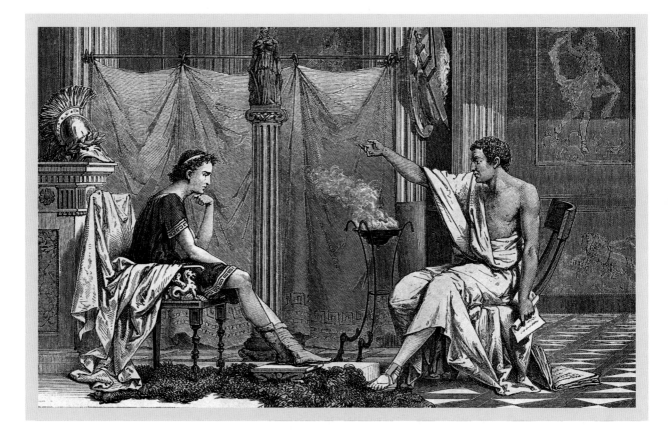

Aristotle served as a tutor to Alexander the Great.

astronomers at first focused on solving practical issues, they later considered fundamental questions, such as the size of the earth and the distance from the earth to the sun. In the third century BCE, Eratosthenes of Cyrene calculated Earth's circumference with amazing accuracy. Less than twenty-five years later, the Greeks had designed mechanical devices capable of calculating the positions of the sun, the moon, and the planets with precision. One device, the Antikythera mechanism, shows that the Greeks had an excellent understanding of eclipses and could predict them accurately. The principles underlying its operation were the work of Archimedes, perhaps the leading scientist of ancient Greece. Archimedes made substantial contributions in astronomy, mathematics, and physics, and made hundreds of scientific discoveries.

Greek technology was equally remarkable. By the late sixth
century BCE, Greeks had developed cranes to aid construction
projects. Wooden winches and pulley hoists were later developed to
lift heavier loads. To aid in the construction projects of the Classical

*Many of Archimedes's
discoveries are still
used by scientists and
mathematicians today.*

Age, the wheelbarrow was invented to transport materials. The Greeks also made numerous military innovations. In the fifth century BCE, they developed a handheld crossbow, the *gastraphetes*, and later other bows that could be fired on horseback during battle. The Diolkos trackway across the Corinthian Isthmus, though primarily an aid to merchant ships, was occasionally used to quickly move warships between the Saronic Gulf and the Gulf of Corinth.

The gastraphetes and other military technology made the ancient Greeks even more effective in battle.

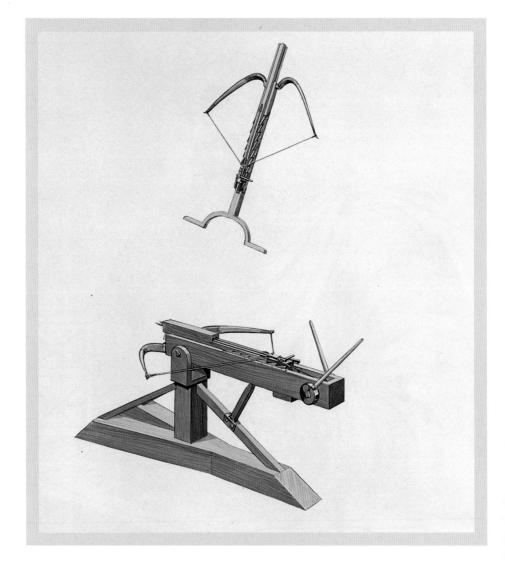

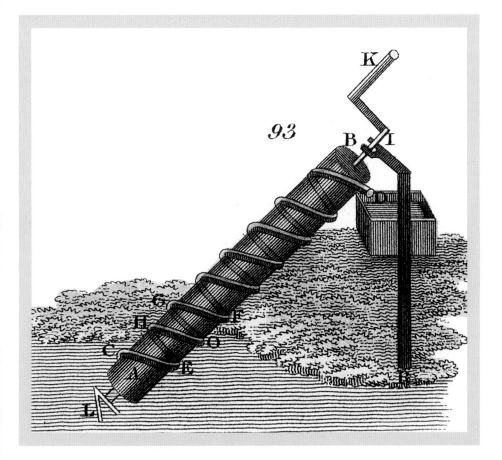

The Archimedes screw was an ancient Greek device used to pump water.

The Greeks developed water mills and water pumps, which were used to fight fires. Waterwheels driven by oxen were employed for a variety of purposes. Archimedes brought the three-masted ship into existence and developed a screw mechanism for efficiently pumping out **bilgewater** from ships.

Through the use of canal locks, the Greeks improved the Egyptians' Canal of the Pharaohs, which connected the Nile River to the Red Sea, and they pioneered the dry dock at about the same time. They developed more accurate clocks. Many of these innovations helped to solve the unique challenges arising in colonial outposts. These innovations stood as symbols of the power of the imaginative Greek mind.

bilgewater (BILJ-waw-tuhr) filthy, stale water that collects in the lowest part of a ship's hull

CHAPTER SIX

THE LEGACY OF ANCIENT GREECE

The Roman Republic's destruction of the wealthy polis of Corinth in 146 BCE signaled a fundamental shift in Greek history. Rome ruled Greece through Macedonian

General Lucius Mummius led the Romans in the destruction of Corinth in 146 BCE.

governors and soon imposed heavy taxes. By the first century BCE, city-states suffered under Roman rule. Despite the admiration of some Roman emperors for Greek culture, Greece received few benefits politically or economically. Local populations were often forced from their homelands, and local cults were overturned. Rome laid claim to Greece's cultural heritage, translating works of art according to Roman standards.

Emperor Nero, sensing the hostility of a defeated Greece, restored its self-governance briefly in 66 CE. By the time of Emperor Trajan's rule (98–117 CE), Athens and Sparta sent representatives to the Roman Senate. Trajan's successor, Hadrian, wished to restore some of the greatness of classical Greece. He established a grouping of cities, the Panhellenion, with Athens at its center. The cities argued constantly, however, and the Panhellenion was soon disbanded. During this time, Greece was undergoing important changes. People were leaving the countryside and flocking to cities. Some of these urban centers prospered and became important cultural centers. Others struggled.

Nero served as emperor of Rome from 54 to 68 CE.

The spread of Christianity throughout Greece and the destruction of local cults spelled the end of traditional Greek polytheism. At the end of the fourth century CE, the Visigoth king Alaric led an assault on Piraeus, the port city of Athens. He laid waste to Sparta, Corinth, and other important urban centers. Emperor Justinian's closing of the Neoplatonic Academy in 529 is usually taken as the endpoint of ancient Greece, although it had effectively come to an end sometime before. With cities in ruins, its population crushed, and its religion waning, Greece's splendor seemingly had disappeared. Centuries later, it would flower magnificently on other shores.

Alaric and his men captured several of ancient Greece's major cities.

RENAISSANCE AND REVIVAL

By the late thirteenth century, a number of factors helped revive the artistic, literary, and philosophical traditions of classical Greece in Italy. Italy in the late Middle Ages had many established cities, most dating back to the Greco-Roman Age. The ancient ruins in those cities reminded the residents of a rich heritage in the distant past.

The Past Is Present

THE VOICE OF THE PEOPLE

When Athens's tyrants were expelled in 510 BCE, Cleisthenes won the subsequent power struggle with the assistance of ordinary citizens. Cleisthenes recognized the wisdom of reshaping the city-state's aristocratic institutions. He devised a new political form, called direct democracy, which gave greater liberty to citizens. In this form of democracy, people voted on issues directly. For the first time in history, citizens had a voice at public assemblies, and the reins of government would be placed in their hands. Direct democracy would be impractical in a nation as large and heavily populated as the United States. But Cleisthenes's groundbreaking concept did serve as the basis for the representative democracy of the United

States in which people vote for representatives who then vote on issues. To this day, the ideals of Athenian democracy still shape modern representative governments.

Italy was not politically unified, but rather divided into several city-states. These city-states had some democratic institutions, and had an influential and wealthy merchant class that assumed political leadership and support of the arts. Italy's leading cities prospered because they were also great trade centers. Cities such as Venice and Florence became fabulously wealthy. Trade on a large scale brought together

Italian cities such as Venice captured the spirit of ancient Greece.

Leonardo da Vinci's Mona Lisa is one of the most famous artworks of the Renaissance.

many intellectual traditions and provided the money necessary to fund large-scale artistic projects.

The sophisticated climate of these cities also produced men whose talents fueled the rebirth of classical learning. Those men looked to the achievements of the past for inspiration.

Scholars—actively reading original texts in poetry, grammar, ethics, and history—assimilated the values of ancient Greece. This revival of art, literature, architecture, and learning was called the Renaissance.

In addition to reviving Greek philosophy, the Renaissance also breathed new life into Greek science and technology. In about 150 BCE, Greek astronomer and geographer Hipparchos invented the astrolabe for measuring the altitude of the sun and other heavenly bodies. Renaissance scientists adapted it for maritime use. Similarly, the dry dock, which first appeared in Egypt during the Hellenistic Age, was used again at the end of the fifteenth century to build England's Portsmouth Naval Base. Renaissance scientists outfitted the Archimedes screw with a crank to improve its efficiency.

Renaissance builders drew consciously on elements of classical architecture. The architectural grandeur of Athens's Acropolis, home to the Parthenon and other temples, inspired Renaissance architects and city planners. The Greeks' elegant sense of proportion and balance guided Early Renaissance masters such as Filippo Brunelleschi and Leon Battista Alberti.

The Greek Revival in America caused renewed interest in grand oratory during the mid-eighteenth century. Men recognized as the most eloquent speakers of their day utilized techniques perfected in the ekklesia at Athens and taught in its schools. By the middle of the nineteenth century, some of America's most influential political leaders were also accomplished orators. Historians have suggested that Abraham Lincoln's Gettysburg Address displays striking parallels with the great funeral oration delivered by Pericles to honor the dead during the Peloponnesian War.

OUR DEBT TO ATHENS

Because Renaissance thinkers, artists, and builders looked to ancient Greece for instruction, we have all felt the influence of their civilization. When we look at buildings designed with balance or with grand columns, we sense the ancient Greeks' devotion to order and reason. Next time you see one of these buildings, learn about an upcoming election, or get caught up in the excitement of the Olympic Games, remember that we owe all of these things to the ancient Greeks.

The Gettysburg Address is one of the most well-known speeches in U.S. history.

BIOGRAPHIES

ALEXANDER III (ALEXANDER THE GREAT) (356–323 BCE), king of Macedon and son of Philip II, extended Greek cultural influence from the Adriatic Sea to the Indus River in a series of military conquests. He is considered one of history's greatest commanders.

ARCHIMEDES (CA. 287–212 BCE) was a brilliant mathematician, engineer, inventor, and astronomer. He designed numerous innovative machines, including the screw pump that bears his name and a "heat ray" that was used to focus the sun's rays onto enemy ships, causing them to catch fire.

ARISTOTLE (384–322 BCE) was an influential philosopher, a student of Plato, and teacher of Alexander the Great. His writings, especially in the sciences and logic, were influential in the Renaissance.

CLEISTHENES (CA. SIXTH CENTURY BCE), successor of Solon, is sometimes called the father of Athenian democracy. His reforms altered local political alliances that had stood for generations and brought ordinary citizens fully into the day-to-day workings of government.

DRACO (CA. SEVENTH CENTURY BCE) was an Athenian lawgiver who drew up the city-state's first written constitution. His laws, which replaced earlier oral traditions, were very harsh; even minor crimes were punishable by death.

ERATOSTHENES (CA. 276–CA. 195 BCE) was an astronomer, cartographer, and geographer who answered fundamental questions about astronomical distance measurement with startling accuracy. He created a map of the known world, calculated the tilt of Earth's axis with precision, and ascertained that the length of a year was 365¼ days.

HOMER (CA. EIGHTH CENTURY BCE) is recognized as the greatest ancient Greek epic poet and is the author of two of the world's most enduring literary masterpieces, *The Iliad* and *The Odyssey*. His works represented the cornerstone of education in ancient Greece and have had an enormous influence on Western literature.

LYCURGUS (CA. 800–CA. 730 BCE) was the legendary Spartan lawgiver who reformed the city-state's constitution, requiring military service of all citizens.

PERICLES (CA. 495–429 BCE) was a leading orator, statesman, and general. A dynamic leader, he furthered the development of democracy in Athens and supported the building of the Parthenon, Greece's greatest temple, during the height of the Classical Age.

PLATO (CA. 423–CA. 347 BCE), a remarkable Athenian philosopher, wrote numerous dialogues that caused readers to think and analyze moral and philosophical problems. He started the influential Academy in Athens and is now most remembered for his *Republic*, which studied the issue of what constituted an ideal government.

SOLON (CA. 638–CA. 558 BCE) was an Athenian legislator who rewrote Athens's constitution, replacing most of Draco's harsh laws with less punitive ones. He tried to reach a better balance between the political power of aristocrats and common citizens.

SOPHOCLES (CA. 496–405 BCE), a playwright of enduring importance, was the greatest writer of tragedies in his time. His *Oedipus Tyrannus* and *Antigone* have broad influence in theater to this day.

TIMELINE

CA. 1200 BCE:
*The Mycenaean palace at
Pylos is destroyed by invaders.*

1627 BCE:
*A volcano on the
island of Thera
erupts, destroying
Cretan palaces and
Minoan settlements
on Santorini.*

128,000 BCE	1800 BCE	1700 BCE	1600 BCE	1500 BCE	1400 BCE	1300 BCE	1200 BCE

**17TH CENTURY
BCE**: *An earthquake
destroys palaces
on Crete.*

128,000 BCE:
*Settlers establish
communities on Crete.*

1450 BCE:
*Earthquakes and
Mycenaean invaders
bring the Minoan
world to an end.*

724 BCE:
Sparta, victorious in Messenian War, enslaves helots.

776 BCE:
The ancient Olympic Games begin.

632 BCE:
Alcmaeonids are expelled from Attica.

1100 BCE	1000 BCE	900 BCE	800 BCE	700 BCE	600 BCE

1100–800 BCE:
Greek Dark Age

750–500 BCE:
The Archaic Greece period.

CA. 750 BCE:
Lycurgus reforms the Spartan constitution. Greek colonization of the Mediterranean begins.

CA. 700 BCE:
Chalcis and Eretria battle for the Lelantine Plain on Euboea.

621 BCE:
Draco gives Athens a written constitution with harsh laws.

499–449 BCE:
The Greco-Persian
Wars are waged.

(timeline continued)

480 BCE:
Xerxes I invades the
Greek mainland.

431 BCE:
Sparta attacks Athens.

431–404 BCE:
The Peloponnesian
War is waged.

508 BCE:
The democratic
reforms of
Cleisthenes
begin.

405 BCE:
The Athenian
navy is destroyed
at Aegospotami.

500 BCE	400 BCE	300 BCE	200 BCE	100 BCE

323–30 BCE:
Hellenistic Period

430–426 BCE:
Disease ravages Athens.

240 BCE:
Eratosthenes
calculates Earth's
circumference.

146 BCE:
The Roman
Republic defeats
Greece at the
Battle of Corinth.

477 BCE:
The Delian League is formed to
confront the invading Persian army.

490 BCE:
Persian king Darius I invades
the Greek mainland.

CA. 150 BCE:
Hipparchos invents
the astrolabe.

594 BCE:
Solon's reforms lay
the groundwork for
Athenian democracy
under Cleisthenes.

500 BCE:
The first schools appear.

500–323 BCE:
The Classical
Greece period.

CA. 1820–CA. 1860 CE:
Greek architecture becomes popular across Europe and North America during the Greek Revival.

CA. 1450 CE:
The Renaissance begins in Florence, Italy.

500 CE   **1000 CE**   **1500 CE**   **2000 CE**

1896 CE:
The modern Olympic Games are staged for first time, in Athens.

529 CE:
Justinian I closes the Neoplatonic Academy.

2012 CE:
After experiencing a severe financial crisis, Greece holds elections to form a new government.

GLOSSARY

abstract (ab-STRAKT) based on ideas rather than things you can touch and see

archaic (ahr-KAY-ik) from the past and not used anymore

bilgewater (BILJ-waw-tuhr) filthy, stale water that collects in the lowest part of a ship's hull

cult (KUHLT) the religious worship of a specific deity

drought (DROUT) a long period without rain

famine (FAM-in) a serious lack of food in a geographic area

fortified (FOR-tuh-fyed) stronger and providing better protection from attack

helots (HEL-uhts) members of a class of serfs in ancient Sparta

inscribe (in-SKRIBE) to write, carve, or engrave letters on a surface

isthmus (IS-muhs) a narrow strip of land that lies between two bodies of water and connects two larger landmasses

legacy (LEG-uh-see) something handed down from one generation to another

maritime (MAR-i-time) having to do with the sea, ships, or navigation

mentor (MEHN-tor) a wise and trusted adviser

mercantile (MUR-kan-tile) relating to trade

opium (OH-pee-uhm) a powerful drug made from poppies, from which heroin and morphine are made

pantheon (PAN-thee-ahn) the gods of a particular mythology grouped together

polytheism (POL-ee-thee-iz-uhm) the worship of or belief in more than one god

Renaissance (REN-uh-sahns) the revival of art and learning, inspired by the ancient Greeks and Romans, that took place in Europe between the fourteenth and sixteenth centuries

rhetoric (REHT-ur-ik) the art or study of using language effectively and persuasively

rituals (RICH-oo-uhlz) acts or series of acts that are always performed in the same way, usually as part of a religious or social ceremony

successor (suhk-SES-ur) one who follows another in a position or sequence

symposium (sim-PO-zee-um) a party with wine, music, and conversation

FIND OUT MORE

BOOKS

Hightower, Paul. *The Greatest Mathematician: Archimedes and His Eureka! Moment.* Berkeley Heights, NJ: Enslow Publishers, 2009.

Hull, Robert. *Ancient Greece.* New York: Gareth Stevens, 2010.

Kerrigan, Michael. *Greeks.* Tarrytown, NY: Benchmark Books, 2010.

Napoli, Donna Jo. *Treasury of Greek Mythology: Classic Stories of Gods, Goddesses, Heroes & Monsters.* Washington, DC: National Geographic Children's Books, 2011.

Villing, Alexandra. *The Ancient Greeks: Their Lives and Their World.* Los Angeles: J. Paul Getty Museum, 2010.

Visit this Scholastic Web site for more information on Ancient Greece:
www.factsfornow.scholastic.com
Enter the keywords **Ancient Greece**

INDEX

Page numbers in *italics* indicate a photograph or map

ABOUT THE AUTHOR

Peter Benoit is a graduate of Skidmore College in Saratoga Springs, New York. A lifelong learner and avid reader, he balances his time between writing and tutoring students at all levels in mathematics and the sciences. He has written dozens of books for Children's Press on topics as diverse as ecosystems, Native American tribes, American history, and disasters. His interest in the classical world began early with reading the Greek and Roman myths as a primary school student. He began to study the history and literature of the classical period in high school, and continued in college. Peter lives in Greenwich, New York.